Love Outlandish

Love Outlandish
Barry Dempster

For Karen,
with admiration!
Best wishes for the
best of words
Barry
July 2009

Brick Books

Library and Archives Canada Cataloguing in Publication

Dempster, Barry, 1952-
    Love outlandish / Barry Dempster.

Poems.
ISBN 978-1-894078-70-2

        I. Title.

PS8557.E4827L58 2009   C811'.54   C2008-907011-9

We acknowledge the Canada Council for the Arts, the Government of
Canada through the Book Publishing Industry Development Program
(BPIDP), and the Ontario Arts Council for their support of our
publishing program.

The cover image is "Jocasta" by Tony Scherman.

The author photograph was taken by OMN Photo Art.

The book is set in Minion and Bliss.

Design and layout by Alan Siu.

Printed by Sunville Printco Inc.

Brick Books
431 Boler Road, Box 20081
London, Ontario N6K 4G6

www.brickbooks.ca

"In a way that leaves
a scar, I
no longer wish to love."
                        — Franz Wright, "Progress"

"Informers inform, burglars burgle, murderers murder, lovers love."
                        — Jean-Luc Godard, *À bout de souffle*

Contents

Love Outlandish

He has his cacti, some of which
resemble minarets, others
something alien and many-

armed. She has her horses, furious
prancers, weekly rides through the forest,
miracles underfoot. So many

people, passions: stamps lovingly
teased from tongues, wine bottles dusted
like babies' bums, Sunday painters

fevered with sunsets. When does joy
become obsession? A friend flips through his
jazz collection, the plastic clatter a mix

of bebop and angel-speak.
A neighbour has planted herself
in her garden, a shape-shifting bloom.

And me, with my film books, my poetry,
my ton of trivia, how did I find
space for you, love

outlandish, first and final thought?
I am gathering images of you and
pasting them on my nakedness, like one

of those street poles in Paris
where possibility is many layers thick.
I am designing a diorama:

a drum roll, a daguerreotype,
an annotated list of dreams
come true. Just like the guy who's mad

for Elvis, a houseful of Andy
Warhol walls and blue suede shoes.
Or the gal with cookbooks on her shelves

instead of food. It's not necessities
that keep us alive, but drawers filled
with butterflies, art deco prints,

Royal Albert teacups, the variety
of smiles that have transformed
your lips into collectables.

Devotion

It was a left turn at Bad Luck, then
a sharp right on Despair, my father
racing to my mother's rescue,
steering wheel spinning, tires skidding,
his happiness sliding out of control.
He picked up her hand which lay in her lap
like a heap of mousy bones
and, lifting it to his lips, kissed the abyss.

The strawberry freckle on her left
ankle, the wrinkled cleavage, the bald spot
where even the hairdresser ran out
of miracles, he sat and memorized
by the hour. *You are my wife*, he
explained, tracing a vein that ran on
and on like a coastline. Love
in absentia, like chrysanthemums
still glowing on Mona Lisa's cheeks,
glissandos between Monk's shadowy fingers.

The body decorative, the body
destroyed, he held her long after
her death date had weathered, held her
in the cluttered corners of his own brain.
Nights when TV was doing its damnedest
to distract him, I'd hear him talking
above the din, telling her how it felt
to be skinned alive. *Love you, love you,*
the old refrain, his hand sitting beside
him on the couch, squeezing air.

Mating

I didn't know the red-winged blackbird
could flick his voice into a tinkle,
the sound of a Lilliputian dinner bell.
So I watched him in the rushes, the way
he shimmed his beak with air and, sure enough,
that ting, silvery and skittish.
Once, twice, head cocked like a puzzle piece,
listening for an even smaller echo.
Could a mate be far away?
Just an inkling of her had turned
his throat into a perfect stroke,
crystal on crystal.

Why do I bother opening my mouth
when it's the same old screech every time?
Asking for love twisted into a cry for help.
So complicated, all the sex stuff,
the cad whistling his head off, begging
like a limp dick to be reassessed
in a kindlier light.
It's not like I'm lurking in marshes
polluting the mist,
but feeling predatory nonetheless
with my too-tall hopes.
Take me in your wings, I shriek,
my voice disguised as a nest of broken twigs.

The cats just howl, an all-clear orgy call.
And the dogs snort and snuffle
as they prime each other's bums.
Lord knows what the bug-eyed flies do –
probably some variant of buzz.
Gets me thinking cross-species thoughts:
what would it feel like to hold
a spider in my rented arms,
or kiss a snake?

Would it turn a red-winged blackbird on
if I wore bells on my fingers
and let the breeze play through?
What's a man to do
when his loneliness can't sing?

A Bestiary

The Rabbit

One blotch of shadow seeps into her cage, then another,
until the wood chips and the water bottle begin to
disappear. Won't be long before night makes her
invisible as well, whiskers, ears, even the white
of her coat. No more humans looming, sticking
their fingers between the wires. No more
children's crushing arms. Just her and the darkness,
cuddled to a oneness, like breath and air. Oh,
the luxury of stretching into space, bits of her
streaming from the cage in tiny squares. Is that
a feast of carrot in the corner or her own heart
finding yet another expanse? The softness
of the question mark tickles her throat, a moan
like her lover makes when he's everywhere at once.

The Hyena

The one thing she hates to eat is modesty, even
the word turns her stomach. She tosses
back her head and barks just long enough to
flaunt her limber oesophagus –
a darkness more delicious than zebra flesh.
Don't get her wrong, she's no narcissist, no
fancy swaggerer. She knows she's ugly, the jungle
version of car exhaust. But nevertheless
perfection: fast, furious. Scavenger, assassin,
swindler, whatever it takes. Isn't survival the
ultimate love affair with the world? She'll eat
sandstorms if she has to, or good old bleached bones.
At the measly lake, lapping up her own reflection,
it's she herself giving the water its sweet, sweet taste.

The Horse

All he can focus on is Velvet's magnificent tail,
a flurry of black sparks transforming the trail
from mere muck and shit into a parade
of darkness. If he trots close enough, her hairs
prickle his nose. If he rears his head, it's like
he's breathing through her follicles. Talk about
erogenous zones, his nose a superior penis, sniffing
the shyness from each blade of grass, inhaling
the whole of Velvet's body, a cloud of oat sweat,
cunt, and sugar cubes. The satisfaction of the snort,
nostrils wide and oily. He is smelling the dust
behind her knees, the indent in her muscle
where the saddle squeezes, the furry patches
inside her ears, his sinuses a wish list of thrills.

The Bull

Baby, he says to the walls of his stall, to
the tiny dust clowns swirling around his hooves.
A bull needs all the practice he can get,
with his thick rope of a tongue, and those
cumbersome lips. Without finesse,
Baby could so easily be a belch.
Ride me, tie me, might do for some, but every
smart bull knows cowboys are anything but crass,
soft and sentimental as the fuzz on a cactus,
in love with the idea of wild. He knows a bull
can never be just an idea, but maybe, *Baby*, with
the rider's thighs wrapped around his flanks and
the rider's nerves melting into sweat, this one will hold
on through the foreplay, come instead of go, a real man.

The Tiger

She pisses here, pisses there, from the creaking
thorn tree to that clump of tall brown grass,
it all belongs to her. And, of course, the
mongoose in the middle. She's crazy about
that mongoose, the ache of him in her glands.
Not to mention the grit and pebbles, and
the tufts of weed, and the blue butterfly that just
happened to cross the piss line. And the slightly
yellow haze in the air, that's hers as well –
she twitches for it in her dreams. Humans
call it territory, silly humans, more inane with
each new definition. This is her essence, now
there's a clever word, whispered to Adam by the first
tiger. *Essence*: everything she is in one brief purr.

Picnic

Grass is growing between my fingers,
treating me like dirt. An army of ants
flexes its thread-like muscles,
measuring the heft of me, the bits
and pieces of my dissolution.

Where my eyes are useless beads of blue glass,
worms squirm with impatience.
This might seem like some sort of *National
Geographic* picnic: tiny, one-track minded
carnivores bred to outlast

both me and my chicken wings
well on our way to extinction. But
I like to think of it as a more
loving process, the grass and I
holding hands, filling each other's spaces.

Just think, an ant toting one cell
of shed skin, savouring a memory
so miniscule it's barely a flicker.
By the time the maggots arrive
in their white priestly gowns, it will be

an intimacy beyond candlelight
and raw-red wine, a consecration
of the lowest and highest minds,
one lone desire devouring everything
except the need for more.

These are not suicidal thoughts,
not a gravedigger's soliloquy,
but a love note tucked under a napkin,
a trail of crumbs falling off the blanket.
I want this in the gaps between

who I am and who I want to be,
the laying on of dew and dust,
hands with their tiny curls of dead skin
touching me in all my newborn places.
I don't want to die, don't be simplistic:

I only want to be consumed
with a gleaming intensity
that feels first and last. What a picnic
we'll have, feasting on every flex,
every writhe and swallow.

Yes

The trouble began when I said yes
to that first sumo push toward a relationship.
It might have been the hot chocolate,
or the casual perusal of the town's one poetry shelf.
Innocent enough, nothing cardiac involved,
just small-talk metaphors
and a *like* let loose in the late winter air.

Yes, most of what we said was true.
Thrill of words spilled into verse.
The comfort of hearing voices coming from
someone else's skull, sharing the craziness.
The lines we read out loud
like litanies of some brand new worship:
The Holy Simile, or The Temple of Buried Rhymes.

And soon I was agreeing to daily calls,
expectations stripping me of those
cautious words like *don't* and *later.*
Depending on it, yes, the wait, the tremble
in the air as the phone finally rings.
Facing faith again, its jostle in the birdcage,
the empty swing that still dangles back and forth.

As a child, I was too lacquered in loneliness
to even dream it left behind.
But now I leap from its flimsy arms, grab
your elbow, drag you to a distance
where you start to fray and almost tear.
Brave, yes, maybe stupid, multiplying hope
as if the zero at its core were full of secret codes.

Is such fracas a form of love?
Sometimes my yes is so cleverly disguised,
you'd never recognize the hero inside.
The fear now is that you'll go away,

a higher echelon of trouble, the kind
that throws hearts from the tops of high rises,
then counts the silences between gasp and crack.

When I said yes to chocolate,
I was surrendering to everything: the greet,
the wrestle, the slow rip that ultimately
becomes a scar. This is the nature of accord.
Standing here in the poetry section,
open to all the lines, all the life-changing
metaphors; nodding discoveries, sharing a face.

It All Starts

It all starts on the edge of the bed,
a man in boyish underwear
rubbing his knees, noticing

his toenails need clipping,
wondering if he might fall
out of love with you today.

Is this yet another poem about you?
No wonder he prefers you
on the telephone

where he can imagine your body
blossoming in ways it never does
when you're beside him on the couch,

reaching across the pillows
to squeeze his hand,
the mime equivalent of a friendly smile.

He's had enough polite, it's stuck
on a ledge in his throat;
he wants passion, fingers clenched,

a risk that rises from a blush.
This isn't just another plea for sex,
but a need to share with you

how cold the floors are
in the morning, how loss pools
around his ankles and gently tugs,

how one desire less might be enough
to redirect the sun, to send
midnight reeling back across the sky.

Just friends, you said so long ago,
like a joke explosion in chemistry class,
as if love came in differently coloured clouds:

the safe kind, the daring, the one that runs.
Is it ever possible for two people
to want the same thing?

He could sit on the edge all day,
pretend you're here beside him,
doing your own dawn routine.

But no, today is the day he loves you
in spite of – or has he got that wrong
and today is really the end of all schemes?

The Phone Rings

Brringg, like the trill of an upstairs maid
in an opera about betrayal.
She is bidding you to destiny:
a mezzo-soprano huddled in
a torn velvet cape, or a handsome tenor,
envelope clutched in his cold fingers.
Once upon a time your life would have been
a glorious melodrama, not this
cut and paste. The phone
turns out to be a salesman in disguise,
a dental reminder, an old aunt
who just wants to say *hi.* Where's your secret
paramour, your plot twist? That last hang-up
came as close to reverie as you can get.

The tension continues, a high note
cracking a wine glass in the dining room hutch.
A demand for your busy wife. A friend
calling to complain about a friend.
A second salesman, his larynx dipped
in wax. You hold your breath through
each exchange, stifling the impulse to swear, or
scream some unrehearsed refrain like, *Do I
know you?* – an orchestra squashed into
one vast cacophony. Somehow you've
become desperate and needy, the strangled screech
of a clarinet. It's getting so you're afraid
to say *goodbye,* even to a dial tone,
that least musical of hopes.

And then one day the *brringg* seems seductive,
a stage whisper from the chorus, a gypsy
with rings on her fingers. You pick up
the phone as if it were a rumour,
a *psst* from the composer, a lump
of wire and plastic transformed into song.

Finally, a fit, the perfect squeeze
of your wife, or your mother risen
from the dead, or a saviour who can't wait
another second to introduce himself.
The right voice at the right moment, there's
crescendo. One note, one held *hello*,
a favourite aria, all swoop and shiver,
the birds and beasts singing the anthem of your name.

A Piece of the Rocky Mountains

She hands me a stone, a piece
of the Rocky Mountains, something
to love. I almost pull my palm
away, say, *Thanks, but I've already
got a lover,* picturing one of your
body parts between my slippery fingers,
the smoothness of your shoulders
as they plunge into the dark of me.
Will a stone last longer than this –
what should I call it – temporal
bliss? Is granite more faithful
than flesh? The Rockies flex
their hard, hard muscles,
centuries with barely a budge.
I hold the stone the way I would
eternal life, a grasp on the verge
of exploding. This is more than
I can accept, desire upon desire,
filling in all my spaces, a sudden
mountain range spilling across
the landscape of my fragile will.
There are gifts we live up to,
and gifts we simply spend.
Hand in hand, stone in pocket,
relationships as tight as knuckles.
Can I love it all? Can I take
relentlessness and still trust
my own brevity? Can I grasp
the smallness of your shoulders
without falling into a lesser place?
Stone held in the same hand
that holds your wrist, a piece of me
engaging with pieces of everything else.

The Goat

– after Edward Albee

I'm in love with a goat, the actor confesses to the actress with just
enough artifice to keep us sane and sitting down. I may be the only one
who wonders if the hair would be wiry or soft, if a tail is something I
could get used to like a love handle or a birthmark, if those rectangular
brown eyes have subtleties I've never considered before. A *baa* or a bark,
I'm not sure what to listen for, but I imagine the breath ragged and
sweet like lightly trampled grass, and a trembling that jitters through
the entire body in a maze of hums.

There's a trick I keep failing at: love, lust and longing thrown into the
air like apples, a juggler's feat of focus and blur, a balance constantly
changing. Smashed fruit, empty hands, the very air an aftershock, how
theatrical. I love her fingers, but not her toes. I lust for the way he cocks
one shoulder. Longing for a piece of this, a prick of that, molecules
shape-shifting into all sorts of impossibles, one toss at a time.

But how can you love a goat without leaving everything else behind?
The first whiskery kiss a total commitment. No pretending it didn't
happen, that barnyard stink. The actor trips across the stage and, lo and
behold, there's a meadow, buttercups shining like floodlights. A perfect
day to go too far, to let the inner satyr out, to strip down to blue sky.
I feel so alone, he shouts at the back rows as if we were a wall slowly
caving in. Oh, how I long to be found by the one who is losing ground
with every foolhardy step. The lust that knows no bounds. *I love the
goat in you,* I say, climbing on stage, being seen for the very first time.

Valentine's Day

To say, *I love you*, on Valentine's Day
is like leaping into the body wave
at a Blue Jays' game or snapping a lighter
at a Springsteen concert. Safety in numbers,
economy-pack thrills. A whole day
to express your feelings, to tinker
with them in public like doodads.
Even engagement rings aren't out of place
at the greasy bottom of a Cracker Jack box.
Come on, be bold, get naked, candy
arrows quivering in your ass.

I love you I love you I love you, go
ballistic, say it until you get slapped.
Take her in your arms
and absolutely refuse to give her back.
Dip both hands in his pants and feel around
for pleased. This is a Get Out of Jail Free
day, a second toss of the dice. Some wildcard
between Roll Santa in the Snow and
Hell, Let's Have a Party. Lust on one half
of the oyster shell, lifetime on the other,
one-liners swallowed whole.

It would be an honour to share
an orgasm with you, things you'd swear
weren't meant for twenty-first century ears,
wish lists like badly translated de Sade.
For one day, you're legendary, heart
swelling purple, spelling out the syllables
of your most cherished fantasies. Go
ahead, arch that back, lift that breast,
Cupid with his gift bag spilling over.
One more time: *I love you*,
in oh so many crowded ways.

The Conversation

Some days are sneakers, tramping through
the leaves, slowly getting soaked. Others
are buses, lumbering from pole to pole,
joining dreams with destinations
like a giant Lego set. Today was smaller,

a phone, a friend with the tinny voice
of a pinprick, doling out solace and advice
the way TV commercials offer life.
I love you, he says, or was it just, *Love you*,
the *I* removed like a useless appendix?

Whatever, the earpiece was downright
warm, as if it too had come from deep
within my body. The rest of the phone
fit in my palm like a child's hand, all need,
sticky as a half-licked sucker. We talked

about everything, from the mourning dove
cooing on his windowsill to my forthcoming suicide
where that dove might come in handy, a tender tone.
Days that really buzz always include
the trivial with the profound, that juxtaposition

where the truth bares its blessings. *I love you too*,
I say, watching the syllables squeezed to threads,
the sort of sewing that makes corpses' lips
look so poised. We go on to discuss
the heat, whether devotion is always a sign

of screwiness, or is it true that some people
just get lucky? I'm speaking to the world
through him, my mouthpiece, my messenger.
I'm pledging my very flesh, the dangle
of my shoe, the way my lips pronounce

some words exactly like a kiss. These are
last confessions, for tomorrow is liable
to be a stone skipping across the surface
of a pond, or a shovel digging its own deep hole.
Can't keep track of it all, can't begin to sing

the dictionary's zillion songs. Eventually,
I have to let him morph back into silence.
When I say goodbye, I'm left holding
a piece of plastic, like a stranger's body
once the lust has been consumed.

Blue Rose

I buy a blue rose to describe
and think of Yeats dipping his quill
in an *ah* of ink, hoping that
love on the page would be less painful,
or at least more rakish, something
to shove in a buttonhole and watch
wilt, beauty slowly disintegrating
to a bruise. Next morning, saturated
with longing, I stumble to the kitchen
for a vitamin, a bolster
for my sad veins, and discover
the crystal vase full of blue water,
the rose having traded bodily fluids
all night. It's the unrequited part of love
Yeats and I do so well, the bleeding,
fists full of paper cuts. The tributaries
leading to our brains are wide open,
the very thoughts we think, fantasies of you
bending over to wipe up a spilled drink,
catching a reflection in the puddle
of my complete devotion. The only
way I know how to love is to drown
all those inconsequential colours,
the pinks of modesty and the greens
of being soothed, soak myself
in a lack of oxygen, a gasp
whenever you enter a room.
I realize you might prefer
violets, a neat little poem
with lots of shy adjectives, but
that's not how Yeats sounds to me, all
thorns and bleed, a daunting chemistry
that gusts across the page in bursts of blue.

Yoga Class

It may be just a basement, but it smoulders
with the exotic intensity you'd expect
from Nepal, drizzled with
butter and curry. Candles shimmer
on various shelves like relics of Buddha's
heart, their flames inching up the walls.
And the music is teasing from far away,
as if a sitar were hiding in the furnace room.
Here is where we've come to stretch our spines
and pretend the infinite is possible.
Pretending is a good thing, make no mistake;
it's the beginning of the world all over again,
the whooshes and rumbles, crack of ribs,
whimper of blood as it slowly descends.

Our only requirement is to lie on a purple mat
and be nothing more than muscle. Hardly
sounds like much, but tell that to the maelstrom
of ideas whipping through our heads,
the twitches in our thighs, the pubic hairs
uncurling like prehistoric ferns.
Busy bodies, all screech and squirm.
Chaos in a time-release capsule.
Sure, let's pretend we're coloured flags
waving in the whirlwind, prayers
spraying in all directions, the scattershot
of fate. More than human, than toes
pointed at the ceiling, more than desire
with nothing to do but chase energy around.

We can't avoid the *I* any longer, helpless
in a newborn, get-me-away-from-me kind of way.
Suddenly, I'm the only purple mat in the room,
candle smoke gripping the back of my throat,

brain cells storming like a puzzle that keeps
being thrown in the air. My body won't obey,
is knocking me off balance, knees jamming,
hips spilling, thoughts clamouring for attention.
I want to be a twist of courage pulled straight
as a hero's gaze. I want my clasped hands
to grip my heart, the one and only true embrace.
I want my love for you to rise up
without will or strain, the way breath
turns into air twenty-four hours a day.

We want too much: a basement in the Himalayas,
a cure for ordinariness, a pretend life
where our bodies are composed of candlelight,
each flicker an acrobatic act of love. *Yoga*
is too small a word, but isn't that the same
for *awe* or *hope*, exclamations so thin
they can hardly down a glass of water?
An hour is all we can do, collapsing
in the final corpse pose, the teacher
hushing us with blankets. Being here
and going beyond ourselves
are the same impossible position,
the sitar notes softly colliding, like-
mindedness one long, praise-filled song.

Lack of Light

The weather gods have no respect
for Saturday, trashing it
with sleet and shivers, knocking
the saunter out of it. We speed-
walk from the car to the chocolate shop,
water-stained shoulders, one especially
cold drop slipping past my collar.
How many Belgian Easter eggs
will it take to feel warm and gold
inside? We could sit here for hours,
fiddling the foil wrappers
into tiny gleaming balls,
wondering what it would be like
to tackle an entire bunny,
the hollow kind with yellow marzipan eyes.

Later, in the antique store,
we discover that wood glows
no matter how long it's been dead;
in fact it's much more incandescent
than those trees in the park that just
sway there looking tall and sombre.
It might be possible to
overpower gloom if we were
sideboards or wardrobes. Even that
ugly log-cabin-like bedroom set
has an all-weather sense of
the absurd. I picture you
in maple, blonder than your
usual crankiness. I lift
my heaviness and think *pine*, think
radiance, imagine my
own steady supply of light.

Finally, at the video store
searching for something four-star
to finish off the afternoon,
the sun suddenly *ta-dahs*, all
fanfare and ribbons. The glint
of your hair almost blinds me,
that flourish of blonde again.
Saturday spirit, even
the Giant Tiger waves its
shine across the parking lot.
If new-found hope were a store,
we'd slide there on the sparks of our heels,
spend the rest of our weekend
inheritance. Who knew we were
so dependent on light? That
shadow in the crease of your lips
was chocolate all along.

Glowing

The sky has flung open its bedroom windows today,
clouds curled gold around their silly edges.
A harbinger of spring, even though we haven't
hit leap year yet, and there's sure to be extra snow.
But I don't care, I'm popping hope, I'm radiant,
I'm kicking off my deep, dark boots.
The sun is pretending to be nude,
rolling over the horizon, cheeks
arched pink, irresistible to the touch.

How can I stay angry with everyone?
Optimism makes even my bruises pretty.
She didn't mean to be mean, it was all those
black holes, and surely he'd take back
three-quarters of his words on instant replay.
Forgiveness is a pool of light wobbling on top
of a snow bank, a saucerful of energy.
Love affairs are easier when the day
is pulling butter faces, all that optimistic melt.

I'm almost blind from savouring
when a supporting cast of crows
all at once abandons a tall pine.
Such a flurry of aggression, torture hoods
thrown over a dozen heads, drawstrings
yanked. This is when love becomes a challenge,
scrambling to find the light refracting
between those inky feathers. A shine
is coming, I insist. Spring will save
our tenderness. Blinking away the shock
until my eyelids turn into canaries.

Touched

You touch me. Couldn't be any
simpler than that, the step by step

of a children's book. There we were
in the front hall, a flock of

ceramic geese climbing the walls,
a sheaf of dried flowers stuck

in a pink vase. Your right arm
lifted, brushing against my left

sleeve, curling around my waist,
that dubious space where bare skin

was barely covered by my shirt.
Shivers made a spiral of me,

the shock of being blood and
ache again. I had to lean

against the door, its sage green sheen
cool and elsewhere. Carried

your fingerprints out to the car,
a swirling mess of wind,

the sycamores shaking
their giant heads. I'll be touched

again, just wait, thumb stains
on my biceps, a streak of

star along my bottom lip,
even those warm-blooded

accidents with strangers,
but never quite like this.

What could I do but give it up,
full moon spilling across

the dashboard, the moment
flung into hundreds of sparks,

one of which used to be your hand.

Willingness

The truth knows its way through my body,
this long range of arms, a willingness,
blood pouring a spirit map of veins,

pores opening themselves to an essence
that feels everywhere like rain. Now
that I have your attention, I want

it all, my name unravelled on your tongue
like a spark giving urge to flame, a kiss
that needs no practice. I want the soft

mound of your palm to be a permanent
part of me, a second heart, an extra
knee. I want your eyes deep inside, a sunken

corridor, where even sleep stays wide-
awake. So much want, streamers of the stuff,
a tickertape extravaganza,

bits and pieces of you in all my
bits and pieces. When it comes
down to it, love is seeing things that are

barely there, and being seen, the pink
of scalp beneath a tuft of hair, a glimpse
of *madly* amidst the usual

common sense. The truth knows
the both of us: how much distance
you evoke, how little change

I name and file, the longings
that we've planned so stubbornly
they're almost diagrams. Love is nothing

like an expectation, instead
a *wham* from out of nowhere,
years rippling around us like comic strips.

I want you to stop pretending
and start surrendering to exactly
how it feels: head-on, upside down.

True

Bible bashers swear true love
is right no matter what the cost.
What good is Christ under lock and key?
Like Spiderman with his fingertips waxed.
Show that super longing, those mad leaps,
almighty emotion.
Back in my Brethren days, confusing
desire with salvation –
is this how I started worshipping you?

Love was the all-day, every-day philosophy,
when I was still sane enough
to have a thought process.
I swallow you like something multi,
brimming with goodies I can hardly pronounce.
God, you *are* true, my favourite verse.
Lying in your arms feels cross-like
in a comfy kind of way, a willingness to be raw,
naked and holy, art squeezed from a lonely curse.

Sex is a form of reverence, don't I know,
having named a new shade of pink
in honour of your lips.
And your wrists top my list
of miracles unsung.
I even pray to you when you aren't
listening, just in case.
True, this is going too far, but where else
can a man stand on a ledge and be heroic?

My final act will be to dangle over
somewhere grand, shout your name, and fall.
Back to the faith where you're an ordinary person
and I can brush against you
without all that greed.
Little spider, heart scurrying for asylum.
Just because you can't save me
doesn't mean I won't love you.
Even the leaps that can't get off the ground are true.

Come Live with Me

Come live with me, I'd like to share
this watch that doesn't tick, this
TV set that takes the sickness
of the world and wraps it
in sex and show, this chimney
growing taller with each blast of heat,
this window staring at a dying oak
and calling each loss a gorgeous miss.

I want to live closer to the core of
all my things, the springs and screws,
the blinking lights, the seams that separate
the *do's* from *don'ts*, the gleam
within the shine. I want to be right here
when you find the perfect word
strayed across the line and learn
the courage it takes to face a brand new story.

Please, come live with me, the sun
with its hundred arms, the steam of tea
floating from lips, the damp spot on the pillow
where soul squeezed through. I want
the marrow, the stretch, the stirrings of green
deep within your eyes. I want the house
to catch your flame, soak in your perfume,
surrender its bones to the creak
only your feet can play.

Come live with me, I'd like to share this
death without a name, this breathing
that aims to outlast desire, this wholeness
belonging to the both of us, like the loops
and straggles of a conversation,
or the soft babble of a kiss.

Pieces

Here's the scar on my left palm –
it looks like a picket fence, all that
long-gone pain trimmed to something
almost pretty. And while you're here,
notice the squash of my knuckles,
the ropy tendons on the backs
of my hands, the wispy blonde hairs
that breeze up and down my arms.
See me, goddamnit, I'm a miracle.

Too intense? Too needy, too scared,
too inconsequential, you name it.
If this is a love affair, I'm the entire
string section on a tear, catgut
screeching at a paper moon. If this
is friendship, I'm reed
and spit, a musical splint
keeping cracked heart songs in tune.
If this is you, then it's definitely me.

I'll never forget the afternoon
you reached out and chose my
wrist bone over all other
body parts. Fascinating protrusion,
precious afterthought, a little
apple motif to remind me how
off-centre paradise can be.
I'd never been just a wrist
before, exhilarating diminutive.

Divide me into pieces, hold me bit by bit.
I may look like a wrinkled fist
or a middle finger with a dent
from squeezing a pen too tight,

but there are mysteries worth loving,
longings to be risked. Have you seen
my wing of ilium yet, or my medulla
oblongata? Keep staring, go beyond
yourself, make me whole again.

Nude Scenes

1/

She stretches herself full-length
on the shimmery, big-screen bed,
a puff of ginger pubic hair
springing from the gap in her nightgown,
which first slips, then slides, finally
opening wide, breasts flowing over
a ridge of ribs like peaches. Her nipples
are seersucker, her belly
a small pot of cream. Because this
is a movie, I have lots of time
to describe: a fold upon a fold,
a plumpness, a parting of her short,
almost childlike legs. Desire
and curiosity touch,
like colours in a chemistry set.
Her left foot twists with pleasure,
pointing into the darkness.
The camera steals in on
her shrimp-pink baby toe as it
rises from the mattress like a queen.

2/

I haven't seen you naked
so have to imagine,
which I concede might very well
be one liberty too many.
I undress you the way the camera
strips the light from branches, the way
the glare peels shadows from the sky.
It's your shoulders that bare themselves
first, the blur of extreme close-up,
then your elbows, a certain glimmer
of a slope, ending with wrists and

fingers that look so different now,
like snails lifted from their shells.
I could go on, I will: the moist backs
of your knees, the ass that flattens
just a bit too much, the sex that's so
full of darkness it has to be sensed
more than seen. Your underpants
have left a trail around your waist
that almost looks like teeth. I
refrain from touching, of course, knowing
your preference for distance, how
far away you always try to be.

3/

It only takes a couple of movies
before I start imagining
everyone naked, finally forced to
tell the truth. The actress stretches
and springs, the audience clutching
her light, exposing her
insecurities. Fat thighs and
skinny, scraped knees. Variety
shows of breasts, vaudevilles of eyebrows
and ears, late-night comedy clubs
sagging with bellyflops. In this
sweep of flesh, no one is really
pretty, perfection absurd. Desire
more instinct than intention.
I sit here surrounded by my own
flesh and fantasize a ginger-haired
puffball, the come-on of a golden toe.
And in this secrecy, I slip
a possibility of you,
a curve, a strand of hair,
a nibble barely begun.

I Saw You

I saw you in the clouds today, amidst the puffy white bears
and flying crocodiles, a whipped-up version of you, high
and flighty, wearing your bits of blue like a teenager
showing off his underwear. I caught a glimpse of your heel
as your toes scurried to conceal themselves as ducklings.

And I'm sure that frothy poodle right above my car
was the barely disguised back of your head. What can I do,
I'm smitten with you, the trails of light you leave
on the horizon, the airplane-winks as you sweep towards
the ground. I saw you glimmer in the highway grass,

a glint of glass or metal. I saw the swing of your chin
in the back seat of a yellow Corvette, as if parts of you
were being whisked to some secret location. I saw
the blush of your lips as the stoplight turned a naked
shade of red. I'd have to ditch my car and climb

an embankment to lose you. I'd have to stand
in the passing lane until the wind hollowed me out.
But there's your left hand on the steering wheel, keeping
me straight, your knee on my knee, preventing me
from stepping on the brake. You love the attention, probably

more than you love me. Don't lie, I saw you raise that
eyebrow, pretending it was just branch and breeze. I saw
the bright bleed of your heart on a billboard for life insurance.
I saw the scrambled letters of your name on the North Carolina
license plate, releasing me from all notions of far away.

Spanish Espadrilles

The earth is quaking under my Spanish espadrilles.
Somewhere, a cartload of black olives
overturns, red wine pours from the sky,
a herd of bug-eyed goats bunts the distance,
frantic to scratch their ears against my shins. Longing for
Granada, flipping through photographs, peeling off
my shirt, a pale alternative to the man leaning
on the Alhambra walls, a cluster of almonds
above him slowly relinquishing their green. Is it
bad if I shut my eyes and am instantly somewhere
else? Do I really have to love this cold Canadian
persistence? Sometimes the moment is a mountain road,
sun cresting ridges like a baby's face peering
over the top of a crib, or should I say,
the memory of that road, veers of dust, motorbikes
popping wheelies, valleys somersaulting far below.
In the fantasy, there's always a plate of bread
and tomatoes, a dribble of blonde oil, and
a barelegged woman with an old-fashioned camera
strung around her neck. We're sweating the scene together,
counting the tapas forks, draining the blue bottles,
letting the lack of clouds empower us, a cat's tongue
daubed behind our knees. We're reading Lorca,
something un-February-like, a puddle of blood
balanced on the bed between us, a bowl for the words
to soak in once they've been murdered properly. This
perfect moment carries a glorious violence in its
fingertips, the way the frailest of blossoms
suddenly burst into the leathers of oranges and limes.
We are hot and happy, then we're dying, daylight
falling into the mountain's catch, an *alcázar*
climbing the flimsy heights of shadow before toppling
into the Moorish night. In Spain, we can be

unmitigated history, damned and saved
in the same crush of heat. I put on my espadrilles
the way Dorothy donned those red slippers,
wishing for that other place so blazing
that the real sizzles into smoke tufts
trailing from flamenco dancers' sleeves.

You're the Last Thought

You're the last thought I hail
before heading under,
if noting that your smile
makes me happy
can be considered a thought,
and why not, it's a complex
scrunch of a smile and
worth the effort, cheek bones
seeding blush, chin lifting its
small apple of a self,
lips, those lips again, curling
just a bit, the way dahlias
flex one petal at a time,
each with its own will or,
better said, desire.
Sleep is surgery,
removing distraction,
replacing you with dark fish
and bowls of talking fruit.
In my dreams, I don't dare
love you. There's a difference
between lighting a match
and swallowing the flame.
Better to grow a fin
or listen to an orange
shuck its inhibitions –
these are things that I can
easily leave behind,
that won't get in the way
of writing cheques or
wearing shoes. Love goes
way beyond imagination,
wedging itself between tongue
and spoon. It couldn't care
less if the bananas

are sighing hymns,
or the peaches seducing
each other with soft false
promises. So let me sleep,
stop smiling. Can't you
think up something else to be
besides my happiness?

Dancing

Bruised and clustered,
you hurl your body
into the rage of the music
the way breeze flings itself
into a cloud of bees,
sex slamming against the floor.

The joy of being
all engine, spunk racing
through corridors, elbows
and knees bruising the air,
heart leaping in your eardrums
like a crazy kangaroo.

Before the algebra of bones,
each breath is chemical,
oxygen burning down
those houses of sweat,
the flow of you, searing
glow across the smoky night.

Every motion is a thrust,
a screw, speed busting
the laws of decency,
making you feel deathless
and rude, the kind of boy
who slays dragons with his hips.

It's a wonder you don't
disappear, a lift-off
into flaming outer space,
the atoms of your thighs
whirling into some sort of
other life form, music made flesh.

Sex Appeal

Spangles of flicker, frisked
from the sequins on her blouse,
filling the hallway with what
someone sucky might call fairies,
but I swear is deeper energy
purling from her pores,
swirling through the lacy stuff,
clinging to the rayon/nylon mix,
aiming for the dry morning air,
front door sparking
a four-alarm reminder
that desire looks a whole lot
different in the light.

And what emanations am I
adding to the day, besides my
usual honesty which leaks
from my bent places, insides of
elbows, cracks and lees?
How to distinguish between
a dark creamer of shadow
and a dirty thought
scrambling to climb a stranger's leg?
Men don't long, they lust.
They (he, me) gush
like ray guns, reducing everything
to a vapour, a novocaine spray.

She leaves me with tickles,
my two beaded bracelets
tugging the hairs on my wrist.
The hall stays lit, but like
a stage set during intermission.
Alone, I'm a prop,
like spit on a cock, like

the stop/start action in a fantasy.
I should have grabbed
an empty pickle jar,
trapped a few of those flickers,
spent the rest of the morning
cooling, pressed up against the glass.

Embouchure

Her embouchure, lips around the word
itself, a horn, a French horn, slightly
elegant and absurd, the combination
giving him delicious shivers. The shock
of *I love you*, a complete stranger suddenly
seizing his throat. Those lips, that mouth,
shaping his sense of self. *Darling!* New
name, new him, flung from the clay
of her tongue, lying there beside her,
each rib listed in the book of... *Love!*
At last he is exclaimed, sung, the object
of her most passionate poems, the ones
that have disposed of Daddy and are
on their own, glorious, lips soft and
swollen, spilling breath across the naked page.
A whistle, a sigh, never dreamt he could be
so easily condensed, four letters, the future
a simple bliss of repetition, finding himself
again and again, in the billowing of her cheeks,
the gleaming of her teeth, the glistening spray
of how well he's reprised. No wonder he's
gone silent, giddy as a deaf boy on a carousel.
All he wants to do is savour, sip, and surrender
the beam of his lips to a kiss. This is how
it is, for now, forever, whichever comes first:
living for that call, that music, waking up
and waiting to be described: *My sweet, my mouthful.*
A slip of the tongue, perhaps, but one
that he swallows along with the dark secrets, the
mutters, the daily dose of advice and praise,
his heart growing twice its size, exquisitely
windy, a bloody symphony of balloons.

One Minute

One minute I'm a fraction of you –
your pulse, your thumb – the next
I'm whisked away, a stage manager's
hook crooked around my neck,
hugging me into the shadows.
One minute the future slaps
a spring photo over these winter days,
the next it's torn into tiny green pieces,
diminished to debris. This is what
it's like to live without faith, a seed
that turns into a pebble, a stone
chrysanthemum soaking up the sun
to feed its stubborn greys. I love you;
I run away; these are the tensions
that keep the sky from toppling, the skin
from snapping off my bones, naked
as a heap of clothes still whispering *undress me.*

I long for certainty, every word
spelled out, desire and all its Latin diagnoses.
After all, isn't love a kind of condition?
My own thumb is totally ignored
despite its showy swirls. Unique's
passé. Now I want to be blurred,
smudged to a teardrop, or a stained
pearl, something of secret value,
a quiet chickadee with its wings
wrapped around a poem. Being close
to you feels like living twice. One minute
I'm muscle in the shape of an embrace,
the next I'm empty arms.

Whiteout

There's steam rising off this first snow,
steam floating from me, corkscrew ghosts
swirling with each shovel pass, spine
curling with desire to see naked ground.
Too much covered up in December, all
those blizzards and wreaths. I haven't
seen your bare throat for days, the sneaky
lies of scarves and turtlenecks. No
wonder I can't find my glasses, the whole
week playing hide-and-seek.

In whiteouts like these, desire
could fill a history book. Bring October
back, oh, please. That night on the dock
when the wind picked up my arms
and simply handed them to you.
I want the grass again, the dew
soaking my jeans, the moon orange
and almost rude. I want darkness,
the wall, the end of it all, not this
steamy glow, this ghost eye watching my
every move. I want the savour of a shiver
that isn't already iced half-dead.

Perhaps it's best to aim ahead.
Surely those Antarctic penguins dream
of spring dividing what seems so solid
into islands and then finally the sea.
Standing on a heap of snow, I imagine
melt slowly lowering my anxieties.
Longing for the season when your arms
won't remind me of a shovel's grip
no matter how hard I need to be held.
When all the extremes are revealed,
like frescoes of the Sacred Heart, proclaiming
nothing need ever be concealed again.

Stormed

And the rain falls in a blur
of mourning doves and dirty streaks
on windowpanes. I can barely
imagine the waddling skunk huddled
beneath the garden shed, sniffing

a stink far worse than her own. Or
the cheap-brown rabbits in the bush,
steaming, soaked. Stems bending, blossoms
ripped like regretted tears, leaves limp
and lying in an oily mess.

Worst of all, I can't see you, your
face dissolving in the deluge.
How many days like this make up
a life of cowering for shelter,
both heart and brain dismally dry?

I blink until it's my eyelashes
that are pouring down my face, until
the trees are sobbing and any thoughts
of going outside to play are swept
away, a lost current raising

aimlessness to an art. This waiting
for the storm to end feels like
an opened umbrella in my chest,
spokes digging into secret flesh,
drips of me letting go and dropping

into rubber boots. I'll hardly
recognize you in forty days and
nights, even your pockets drowned, your
eyes stained, too much blue – nothing
for me to hold in my arms but

dampness creeping to a chill. Unless,
right here and now, I storm my way
beyond safe, to the very place
where your fingers are failing to grasp
their own splashes of panic. Together,

we will sink into this new depth,
this rush of foolishness and courage.
Call it love or just plain dumb,
whatever the baby sparrow
becomes when he opens his beak

and quickly fills himself with rain.

Sick with Desire

Sick with desire, I plunge each foot
into the watery sand, desperate
for the thwack and glug that remind me
I'm still on planet earth, that the beach
isn't slowly disintegrating.
So full of want that the breeze
listing across the shallows
almost blows me over. And so I try
to focus, solidify, remark on
the Moorish squiggles of purple and
bronze, the honeycomb ripples, the way
your big toe stretches abandoned footprints
to a secret scrawl. None of this grounds
me, dizzy swell, not even the sandpiper
with his Pinocchio nose
who simply cheeps, *Go deeper, deeper.*
If this were a movie, I'd slo-mo
into the breathing blonde distance, wave
goodbye. If this were a song, I'd build
a sand bridge between verses
that would, of course, crumble
the minute I was gone. But I'm a long drink
of water, a man so out of balance
he scuttles. All I can do
is look down, sidle on, careful
of razor clams, as if avoiding pain
were the whole point.
I'm being good, aren't I,
keeping it to myself, pretending
to tan instead of burning up?
The centre of the universe and I'm slurping –
isn't that some version of my greatest
fear? How can I be here, can I want
one more step? If this were a fable,
I'd turn into a spider crab,
wriggle my blue-barnacled shell

into a hole in the sand.
If this were real life,
I'd screech down like a gull and
steal everything in sight. But this
is just a beach walk, a Cape Cod
stroll. I'm not supposed to want
anything more than the bathed-blue sky
and the promise of tidal logic.
I will keep my hands to myself.
I'll leave your footprints alone.

I'd Like to Lick Your Thumb

I'd like to lick your thumb, I said
when offered a piece of
chocolate chip muffin.
Just a joke, no need for alarm.
Don't go running from the room,
thumb held aloft like a popsicle
in the presence of a tall dog.

I'll keep my tongue to myself,
promise.
And the vision of your thumb
smeared in blonde crumbs
like a doll's head swirled
with perfect curls.
Not a peep about the taste,

salt and chocolate stirred to a creamy
paste, luscious against my gums.
Don't worry, I wouldn't bite,
these are honourable jaws.
But oh, how I'd nibble,
bunny-like, my moustache aquiver,
your thumbprint slowly unravelling

into a long, pink river.
This is all hypothetical,
of course, if I were... if you could...
In reality, your thumb is safe,
symbolic as a flag.
Go ahead, wave it in my face.
I will stand at attention, tongue

rolled to the back of my throat.
Perhaps I'll take that offered piece,
spongy little substitute,
pop it politely in my mouth,
mmm.
Pretend it's the chocolate
I adore.

Oozing

The man in the moon gives one
of those wry romantic grins,
but you're sneezing.
You collapse on the bed,
washcloth spread across your face,
a Cleopatra wilt.
No amount of Miles Davis
will budge you tonight, your body
belongs to the common cold.

Day and night, the dark
forces of biology dog me. And now
you're oozing right before my eyes.
The cat on my lap sweet and fuzzy,
rippling with bacteria
as surely as the damp patches
down my basement walls. Yeasts
in my slippers. Microbes
on my fresh filet of sole.

The Doukhobors had it wrong
when they praised the inner light.
Wiser, the neurotics who sing
every pore as a tiny abyss.
I creep closer to you in bed.
No virus ever looked lovelier.
Just a kiss, a subtle bite, the moon
going green as graveyard grass,
diseases colliding with a squish.

Imaginary Hand

Edmonton. Boxed in the back seat of a cab,
I reach for your imaginary hand,
a little grasp and sinew to balance out
the endless malls, the sprawl of family life.
Not that your hand isn't real, just elsewhere,
left in Ontario counting pages and
punching lucky numbers into telephones.
But you'd be here if you could, a good enough
definition of love, a constant willingness.
So why am I feeling so alone?
Is it lack of love that guarantees
the world its disappointments? I squeeze
your fingers into a ball of bone, feel
your blood coursing through a hollowness
that only pretends to be far away.
This is your thumb, I say out loud,
the cabby muttering, *Eh?* How to explain
how lost I am without you: one more left turn
and our palms slide off the map.
All I can do is hold on to your absence
as if it were a rip in the universe, that
sliver of space the gods slip through.

Between

I love the between of your fingers,
those spaces my own fingers fit.
The way sky slides between hydro lines
or February branches like long,
blue envelopes; the way dead air is
fed with breeze, little dervishes of
dust. A plastic bag swirls
up my driveway, invisible gusto,
just the right mix of want and need. It
dives, it lifts, etc., an emptiness
willing to be tossed. Everything
seen has a hole somewhere,
spilling over with rescues of light.
But damage only lasts a second
before it's overcome, a shadow
play of duck's bills and rabbit's ears,
an ooze of blood making canvas of
a wound, a mirror's constant round
of relationships. You take me by
surprise when you spread your fingers,
stealing me from all those busy visions,
drawing my own *between* from its disguise
as fist. The wind blows, the holes in the world
close, as my thumb begins to open,
my baby finger feeling its first
tug of desire. Such a perfect
fit, as if your hand had been designed
with me in mind, as if the gods had
measured our spaces down to
the last fraction of a wish.

Found

I wake up not touching you,
my right hand like a ball
stranded in the tough, thick grass,
a mere plaything missing its context,
or a weapon waiting patiently
to be disarmed. Earlier, this same hand
slapped your dashboard
instead of striking you,
and later, would hit any open surface,
as long as it hurt.
The opposite of loved is a palm
sanded down to sheen, a wrist
unscrewed, a finger by finger
fade-out. Inches of white sheet
have never seemed so expansive before,
the way a snowfall intensifies
distance. The plunge of your hips
a chasm away, your own hands
tucked around your belly
as if holding something in.
I will never reach you, my nerves
misfiring, a bit of pillow between my teeth.
Except for faith, almost miraculous,
a groove that runs across the mattress
like a rope bridge. I close my eyes
and picture flesh on flesh,
my fist bumping against your elbow,
your heart beating inside my wrist.
Next time I wake, our arms
as entangled as bones can get, I use
my free hand to satisfy a knuckle itch
and end up scratching yours instead.
At first it feels numb, a stunning lack

of matter, but then I realize who
I'm stroking, that as long as I
continue to forget myself
you'll never need to lift a finger,
all your tinglings taken care of,
all your losses found.

A Bad Night

In the worst of a bad night's dreams,
you slap my face before loping
away, a sting that follows me
into wakefulness as if my pillow
were a weave of nettles. Love
and its unconscious betrayals,
my inner self dismantling
all the trust, ripping up the legal
tender. I want you so badly, I want
it over with, the shreds of bed,
the accident imagery, the once sweet
words in a sour sink of ear.

The next day a grey kitten suddenly
appears on my walk through ache and shame,
a sign from the sidewalk gods that
not only does innocence still exist,
it rolls over on its silvery back,
leaving a lovely squirm on the curb.
This I can love anew, cradling
the purr, an optimist's promise,
taking an armful home with me.
Once upon a sleep, you were thin air
too, a pounce from out of nowhere,
that place where real needs begin.

Afraid of another night of dread,
I dally until well after midnight,
reading the same stanza eleven times
at least, ducking the metaphors
that almost qualify as dreams.
I think of Leonard Cohen, pooh-poohing
the idea of a ladies' man, asking
why then had he spent ten thousand nights
alone. Love is no guarantee of

company, the heart far gone, the body
revising its whole notion of
emptiness. Something in my spine
clenches, a tail barely evolved.

When I eventually fall asleep,
I dream that the cricket behind
the cedar chest has crawled up
onto the bed and is singing
my name over and over. Never
expected to become a love song,
a shiny black blip of sheer desire.
As long as I just lie here listening,
you are finally whole and true.
By the time the cricket is wearing
Leonard Cohen's face, I'm ready
to let go, lose everything.

The Argument

He only steps on the blue tiles
as he paces the kitchen and hallway
declaiming détente, the phone tucked

against his left ear and shoulder
like a translation device. The green
tiles are being saved for anger,

just in case he needs somewhere
definitive to stomp. And the white,
well, what if a miracle were

to happen and she finally
understood his secret self, wouldn't
he want a square or two of pure

wonder in which to shed his feet,
already well on his way to
new levels of relationship?

Experts say the heart is clever,
complex, a high-tech toy –
a dependency on tricks, like

an iPod swimming in Sarah
McLachlan songs, or a pager
linking him to every loneliness

in the land. He could have fallen
in love with anyone, if only
he'd realized his options. But

his heart made its impassioned, caveman
choice and now he's stuck on blue, wading
through promises and plans, light bulbs

pulsing hot like they do in cartoons.
If he does this, will she do that,
a guarantee? Marriage is

a contract, after all, as much ink
as flesh. Of course, she will. Love
stretching its legs across a painted

map, straining not to trip or tumble
into jungle greens where suppressed
things have been festering for years.

He works it out because he can't
imagine the future without her,
which either brands him obsolete

or visionary. It doesn't matter;
his heart is playing "Angel" for
the thousandth time. He says something

nice into the phone, then nicer.
By the time he reaches *goodbye,*
its meaning has been changed to

see you soon. Stunned by the notion
that most of these emotions
have lives of their own, he doesn't even

notice he's shifted from blue tiles to white.

After Watching *Miami Vice*

I'd expected the ballsy gleam of guns,
the gruesome head wound wide enough for
two fingers, the couple of car chases
involving bridges and Little Havana back streets.
I'd even counted on slightly shallow,
a break from all the Middle East intensities.
But soulless was a surprise, Sonny and Rico
drilling grates in the darkness,
what bits of light there were swirling like blood
down a drain, a sleek, slippery emptiness.

Leaving the theatre, blinks strobing across
the parking lot, the world drags dismal,
asphalt soft with too much flame, traffic
a jumble of air-conditioned tombs.
Is it any wonder I feel far away from you,
one of us still stranded in Miami?

The real crime had nothing to do with drugs
and delicate blue lines, but with the desolation
of cool, those casual cityscapes, the Gulf of
Mexico reduced to a shadowy wake.
Sure, the bad guys paid, stacks of sins,
but no one found happiness at the bottom
of a stash bag, no one devised a way
to fix the sun's piss-poor rays, to reinvent
the day as something finer than an August dog.

There's a saltiness in the southern Ontario air,
and a sense that this seventh day has more to do
with resignation than rest. I take you home,
one street handing me on to the next,
a pattern of wishes on their way

to pure ennui. Sonny/Rico, nasty
little blank stares. I might as well
be riding in the trunk, dead and
folded meanly in two, someone you
used to love before this dark betrayal,
this temporary vice of forgetting how to care.

The Silent Treatment

How easy it is to say nothing,
here at The Crow's Nest, stirring gnocchi
into swirls of basil butter,
letting all limitations rule.
Strange, that our absences define us,
but they do, like the jagged lines of
darkness around stars. I wish I could
hold your hand, a tether.
Or draw the distance from your eyes.
But these are intimacies, big shudders,
things that touch and truly see.
What's another word for omen,
one that doesn't grab so much?

When I'm not busy with the oily
faces on my plate, I'm looking out
the window, endorsing your
insignificance. Two crows
are getting along much better
than we are, trading wonder back and forth.
And the colour black is having a ball
with it all, inventing subtle
differences to celebrate.

When I finally get the nerve to ask
where you've gone, I realize the answer
is always the same: *away*, the only
word that absence knows by heart.
I've been sitting here alone all this time,
one of the many incidentals
in a busy restaurant – a menu,
a chair across the way,
a mouth to be fed. If only I'd
reached across the table at the start,
learned what it's like to be a crow
faced with all that air, the exact
same emptiness as your gaze.

The Long Argument

We embalm the day in argument,
out amongst the geese at Fairy
Lake, our bitterness embodied
in honks and hisses. Overweight
dogs strain at their leashes, longing
for jaws full of feathers. The only
safety is the fake cardinal
in the baby blue spruce; someone
didn't trust nature, wrapping
the tiny wire legs around
a branch. Further down the path,
a plaque listing all the trees
planted in the park, from larch to
weeping willow. Should we be
ashamed at how few we recognize,
or forget self-improvement
and storm on? The entire lake
encircles us, our mini-maelstrom
sucking down the afternoon.

And so we fight through the early
evening too, stopping just long enough
to agree that the real cardinal
on the back fence is a reassuring
sight. If you were a dog, you'd be
one of those giant poodles
trimmed to pompoms, noticing
nothing but your own stir of air.
I'd be a whippet, all gums and
bones, yapping like a goose.
Guess which one of us would dive
for the other's ankles, and which would
turn a prance into a funeral march?
Notice, there's no mention of love here,

we've simply lost the trail.
You show me yours, I'll show you
mine – the mean red birds
our hearts have become.

Near midnight, Cinderella
complexes set to explode,
we call it quits. I drive home
through a storm that sharpens
on the hills, lightning flashbacks
of another, more vivid life
where every inch of skin shook
with truth and tenderness. By the time
the hailstones are dogging me,
I'm wondering whether we've damaged
our little corner of the eco-
system, let some demons in,
a pack of them, soaked tails dragged
behind like dropped leashes. It takes
a torrent to make me forget
how angry I am, whimpering
as the road gets washed away.
What if I drown in all this sorrow?
Would you plant a floating tree?

Saving You

Another day of saving you, *phew*,
mice tucked away in their cheddar igloos,
moths sprinkled with naphthalene. Even
God can go to sleep, his finger strings

in knots. So why don't I feel
better, as if I'd received a letter
from the Queen commending my Christ complex,
dubbing me essential? What's with this –

small-cap me huddled
in a heap of your greatest misses?
I lie on my back, perfect victim pose,
and wait for the ceiling to spread its ribs,

a bevy of ER angels descending,
lifting me to a new-found shakiness.
I want to be the rescued one, pretty
please. Rip off the strength rune that dangles

around my neck, remove my backbone
through a straw. Falling apart is such
a luxury, one speck of negativity
at a time. Tomorrow, when the phone

does its imitation of a car alarm,
I'll be in pieces, *oops*, drywall carved
into tiny broken hearts, dustballs
deconstructed. *Ready or not, I'm lost,*

you'll say, inviting my answering machine
on a misery quest. But it won't be
me, that sucky voice, that dead air
confessional. You'll have to hang up,

slog across the parking lot to the self-
help section of the shopping mall,
buy a list of platitudes: *What to
Do When Your Saviour Drops the Ball.*

A Distal Winter's Night

A distal winter's night, city-centric,
Yonge Street with its neon bleeds,
snow moths batting the street lamps,
sucking up the light. It's a night
where the homeless are huddled in
doorways, just another pile
of urban shrug. A night where
tires are alive and shopping bags
bang against tone-deaf knees.
A night of steel shouts, of slush
slurring itself into half-dead puddles.

A fight brewing, a night where I long
to tell the truth. You cold city
with your damned black-ice
distances. Shadows
swooping from billboard struts,
feeding on the cracks between sleeves
and gloves. Breezes slashing
from broken glass. Car crashes
and heart attacks. Losers. Those just
lost. Shivers. Sudden stops.

This is the night where you'll eventually yell
at me, and I'll yell back, the wind flinging
syllables into sleety bursts.
There are strangers I feel closer to than you.
Tonight I will actually imagine
walking on without you, turn up
an unfamiliar street, choose a house,
this house, with coach lights and quartz
in the window, now arrange my fist around
the doorknob and twist, a whole new
revolution. The night I will become
the other person, snowflakes darkening my hair.

Rise Up

Dumped on Easter Sunday, as mean
as irony can get. A friend emails
a cartoon of a crucified bunny,
a grimace turning its whiskers
frayed and sweaty. How far is it
from faith to ridicule?
Am I there yet, riding this bronzed turkey
into mashed potato hell, all
the butteriness making me feel slick,
deboned? If ever there was a day
when I needed someone in control,
this is it. Call it heartbreak, call it
hide the egg. Chocolate dark enough
to hide the bloodstains.

Once upon a parable, I had a special one
whose mission was to say sweet things
and help me not to feel dead. *Rise up,*
outdo the daffodils, he'd say, rolling
my fears away. But then earlier today
devotion switched to a dark cliché.
He reneged, strayed, crossed his eyes.
His last kiss still ricocheting
in my ear. And now I can't even pray
for wondering whether Christ had
wimpy moments, if dying for all mankind
would hurt more or less.

Once the grace has been begged
and the feast scoured, it's just me
and the ache. Two thousand years
of thinking about miracles.

If the resurrection angel were to creep in
and rescue me, I'd probably try to eat her,
gold foil sparking against my teeth. Is it more
honest to be alone or is this yet another
wailing stone, another pissed-off pose?
My heart is sinking
cartoon-like in my featherless chest.

Take Care

Take care, you say into the phone,
meaning *go on alone*.
And here I thought caring grasped
as close to heaven as one could get,
some elbow grease and a sudden
blueprint of veins. It took
actual physical presence to rub your back,
to help you wash the mismatched dishes,
to hold one of your poems between my fingers
like a purple butterfly. Nerves, and pores,
and bristling energy, what happened
to being there, doing, stirring the pot?
I think of hugs at the end of a letter,
too small to even fit around my wrist.
Love needs muscle and grip, collarbone
sliding into collarbone, a penny
of sweat on your neck. It takes every
pound of you to hold me aloft,
to rearrange my gravity. You need
arms to really do the job; you need
a steep hill of spine, a set of ankles
keeping trust on its shaky feet.
But go ahead, long for me from far off,
feel the miles tearing like tissue, popping
bones from their sockets, spreading skin
across the nothingness like a treasure map
with Xs stretched into fades. *Take care*.
And here I thought you needed
at least one of my thumbs to zip you up.

Twelfth Grey Day in a Row

Twelfth grey day in a row, the sun
on sabbatical, having itself
a hell of a time, sliding along
a beach, getting creamy and laid,
forgetting we even exist.

We? How communal am I today,
how far can I see in this dour
lack of light? I'm trying to speak
for the whole street, every shade and
slump, but I'm afraid that I'm just
whispering to you again, vanished one,
partner to the lost sun, proof that
love exists even when it stops
casting reflections in the mirror.

Regardless, I took you for a walk
this afternoon, tramping through a bog
of soggy leaves, sharing how little
the world cares for me. At least
I think you were there, a blow of
memory, a sudden flash of
cardinal swooping across the path.

It makes sense, you sun eater, you
blood loss, flying away with the only
colour for miles around. Is it
any wonder that back home I don't
bother with lamps even when I lose
the notion of my own hands. Sitting
in the dark is a soothing lie,
the moon up there in the drab sky
like something that might have mattered,
something I could have based a religion on.

It sends a splash of shadows
across the lawn, on the driveway
with its brief beginning and end,
on a raccoon snuffing the dying
grass for a feast of wriggling flesh.

Wait, is this another incarnation
of you and your hunger for abandonment?
Is my watching a way of whispering
we, we... keeping the exchange alive?
How little I trust myself in
the midst of so much blindness.

Longing to be alone, starkly
sunless, the state of place so
grey even the cardinals have been drained,
and that coon, persistent though he is,
turning out to be just another
shadow thrown on the heap.

Howl

I've been listening to the wind howl
for two days now, a phantom wolf
suffering out behind the garden shed,
nursing a bullet wound or a loneliness
that wasn't inbred and simply can't
be believed. Watch how it hurts
the maple trees to lose their sugariness,
and the proud grass to fade slowly
brittle brown. It hurts me just to
listen, let alone the glimpses of
scrawny limbs and moth-chewed scarves.

As for you, your cheeks are red,
abrasive, yet you're still upright,
unrepentant, which includes a little
wolfishness, sweated on by the moon.
When the time comes to lose you,
it will be a day like this, whipped
and whining, leaves spinning
in the streets like melodrama,
tears forced from my eyes by a tiny
hook. *The world is a harsh place,*
you'll howl, trying to lick the rawness
that surrounds you, disturbed at
having to see me play the role of prey.

You never meant to hurt me, it's just
seasonal, hope hibernating,
futures snapping shut. Forgive me
the howls shaped from my own breathless
bones, the echo whistle of a kiss.
Today reminds me of the end, a place
I've languished in so long that calendars
are useless, days flipping by without order
or resolve, bits of paper eaten by the wind.

So Special

I said, *Move,* and she moved.
Hold me, and she did.
Let me go, and her arms
slipped to her sides like water
disappearing down a drain.
I should have requested Greek
or handcuffs or almond
croissants, seen how varied
devotion could be. The
romance of met needs (sounds like
wet knees): two people/one
self. I said, *Come,* and she came
bursting across the room,
banging into me, shadows
smashed. *Love me, hate me,*
capable of everything,
Cupid with his schizo
quiver, one tip smeared with
lipstick, the other with blood.

Lovers have it easy,
mouthing whatever it takes
to turn double-talk into
proof. *But she made me feel
so special.* Special, like
a green sky, or a duck
with panda bear ears, or
a wave that crashes without
breaking. She said, *Forever,*
when she meant *right now,*
crushing me to her breasts
as if her ribs had x-ray
eyes, seeing through me
to a space where desire
and truth were too naked

to tell apart. The heart
with its royal edicts,
a crown of *mine, all mine.*

I said, *Goodbye,* and she
wiggled her fingers. *Never
again,* and the whole of her
disappeared like short term
memory after a stroke.
I should have demanded
alimony or black
sutures or a reference
letter listing all my
sexy parts in French. Strange,
but the pain isn't
exquisite at all,
a deranged combination
of nausea and terror.
Faith flying out the window
on dozens of tattered wings.
I'll never shout *love* again
(and she probably concurs):
a word like a crack
in a crystal vase refracting
jagged splits of light.

The Heartbreak Hall of Fame

Day three in the Heartbreak Hall of Fame
and I hear your voice again. Actually,
I pick up the phone and you're there,
the way God is supposed to wait
on the other side of prayer. *How's it going?*
you ask. *Appropriately shitty,* I say,
glib with a gun to its head. That's as deep
as we go, surprised to be wading,
tugged by a whirlpool with the frail suck
of a bathtub drain. So how come it hurts
this much? One pain releasing another,
that lifetime supply. Why have I saved
all these Rorschach scars? No wonder
there's so little new info space.
Full of loss, brown bottles of the stuff,
shelves stacked like a substitute spine.
I can rhyme off the names of every slight,
but can't recite a single poem.
How's it going?
It's stuck like an ankle in a gopher's hole,
it's breaking the same old bones.

The Last Photograph

I rip the so-called cherished moment
in two, the glassiness of the past
slippery between my fingers.
Now I'm in one hand, you in the other.
I rip again, dividing you from
your elbows left leaning on the table.
I rip a third time, severing your
shoulder blade, almost shredding your neck.
Again, again, the raspy burr of paper
being torn. Your chest is now
half a dozen pieces, a few fallen
to the floor. Your ex-chair
in tatters, unidentifiable. Which leaves
just your head, a tiny circle of energy,
like one of those beauty marks
I might have pasted on my cheek
were I seventeenth century and French.
Too tiny to properly rip, to crumple.
A fish eye shocked by death.
A bindi turning a forehead into
an x-ray machine. What's left of you
is spit-stuck to my thumb, staring up at me.
I could swallow you, one small roll
of tongue. I could shake you over
the garbage can like a dot of yesterday's
confetti. Or I could simply wear you, scare
the cops when they come to investigate
your decapitation, my thumbprint wearing
your careless smile.

Rumble

Patti Scialfa sings "Rumble Doll" over and over,
my finger poised on repeat. Same old heartbreak and
unworthiness, half-clichéd, drums pounding like one of
those Life Channel heart transplants, all bleedings exposed.
Why am I so susceptible? Give me a third glass
of wine and I'll graduate to Roberta Flack,
those thirty-years-ago sessions for "Ballad of
the Sad Young Men." Not quite so gloomily romantic
at fifty, all feelings crusted with tangles and knots,
although look at Patti, in the middle of it
herself, still looking and sounding game. No wonder
I sing along, beautifully cracked and flat.

It used to be evenings with Janis Ian,
throat turned inside out, a case of near nicotine
poisoning. *I learned the truth at 17*, hell,
was there ever such a measure, heaps of hours,
dreads of days, the accumulation that ends up
history? I'd sit in the big bedroom closet,
practically humping the speakers, her sighs sweet-hot
on the soft skin of my neck, hangers chiming above
like backup singers. Never alone with misery,
I'd join the lip-synching crowd, the fatties and baldies
who've now graduated to karaoke and
second-hand solutions like divorce. The chorus
is a choir, a whole generation lifting
their plangent voices to those broken lights we call stars.

Feeling back, was my love affair with the girl in
psychology class, or with Joni Mitchell blue under
all that blonde hair? Was it Chris I might have married
or Linda Ronstadt's high notes, the way they squeezed into
my chest and felt like small, damaged wings? There was even
a fling with Bryan Ferry, a slavish thing, where
all I wanted was to hear him moan. My mother

was right, music led to sex, blood rushing up and down
the strings, fingertips callused yet blushing. She was
wrong about the drums though, darkest Africa, all
those pagan mumbles. The beat was born in my
own rec room the night I wrestled Janis Joplin
to the floor, pulses played over throbs, thunder
spinning like the wheel of a just-crashed car.

But back to Patti, one last *rumble*. We both know
the heart doesn't really break, just takes on ballast
and too much sad brain. Look at her now, married
to the Boss, trying to forget all those years of
being disembodied. Singing alongside her,
shedding tears in a socially acceptable way,
I'm worthy of any bar in town. And when we've
finally run out of guitars and frowns, the silence
will be cleansing, death-like in its magnitude,
a lament for all the love that slipped away,
all the voices sealed in bottles or shoved
in closets, never to be heard again.

Hard Song

There are no grey songs on the radio,
no ratty little hearts making do.
It's all about loving or hating
some universal you, valves pulsing
with lust or being ripped to bits,
a storm of skin and bone confetti.
The singer sips from an open wound,
a blood bubble poised between his lips.
One song, he's dying, a note pitched
so high it's lost; the next, he's pledging
discovery, a big red kiss
doing its brazen best.

I wonder which kind I sing the loudest,
a sliver of me embedded
in a puffy mound of faith.
Slammed I am, too many times
to count, an angry welt that used to be
my face. I'm up, I'm down, falling
in and out, racing passion
before it crashes, bliss and misery
like Siamese twins joined at the throat.

My favourite is the one where his love
keeps trouncing distance
even after she's gone, making
harmonies out of death rattles.
It's the crack in his heart
where the melody lingers, the hiss
of an old 45. How can I help
but sing along, hard, hard song,
unconditional illusion.

After

The day before we broke up,
we chatted on the phone twice,
watched a movie together, saw
some of the same shapes, shared
a shiver when the sun went down,
thought each other's thoughts –
or thought we did.
Ordinary, I'd say, your hand,
my hand, same texture, same
clasp. While around us, the globe
did its usual tilt and fall, atoms
seething, leaves plastered
to the ground as if they'd found
a way to defy gravity, filling in
some of the distance
between sky and grave.

And then it was the day itself,
sunny enough, but with a rip
of chill. Another telephone
attachment, half-formed sentences
wrecking more than grammar
normally allows, a year's
worth of insecurities
reaming the vowels, twisting
syllables into shots, momentum
taking over in sweeps of wind,
stripping the branches
outside my window, dismantling
anything resembling a comfort
or a dream. Afterwards, I dropped
the phone to the floor, adding
to the weight of debris.

The day after, and after, and
after, words seeping stale.
The same planet,
surprisingly. A man lying
in the ditch on Queensville Side Road,
another well-planted symbol.
And the cow pushing its tongue
through the diamond fence,
brave yet pathetic, trying to eat
air that doesn't belong to her.
I drive to the store three times
that day, forgetfulness swallowing
the most unbearable hours. *Love?*
What a weird refrain. Here
and disappeared. Like everything
ever said.

Lost Love

No grief, not a trace,
just this pointillist vision
of your face. Have you
finally gone to pieces?
Like those dots swimming
in my eyes the first time
I zoomed in for a kiss,
your lips as whole as the sky.

Why have I bothered to
bring you back? This game of
memory fetch. As if
a bit of me has held on,
a mole with its mysterious
pucker, a wrinkle embedded
to the bone, a thread of vein
vanishing in an underground lake.

I reach out and my fingertip
becomes the shine
on the giant surface
of a dime. No wonder
I can't remember something
as grand as the bend in your wrist.
The shattered vision is all mine,
like the kaleidoscope's eye.

Crumbs

My friend's sheltie looks at me lovingly
as I sit there in her favourite chair
unloading my latest list of woes.
This time my heart really is broken, but
frankly she doesn't care, eyeing my plate
with crumbs from a lemon square
I just gobbled between sobs.
We are both unhappy, that much
is shared, but crumbs and heartbreak
are hardly the same staggerings.
Or are they? Hunger makes her belly
feel like doom, my own cavities cold
and heavy as the rooms of the newly dead.
We are both longing for impossibles,
tongues coated with sugar dust. And so what
do I do? I pick up my plate and place it
on the rug in front of her.
She creeps forward on bended paws
and starts licking, a burble that finally
turns into an outright slurp. The crumbs
are gone in an instant, then it's on
to the painted roses and the little frills
that form the circle shape. She devours
the clay, the kiln's killing heat, the very
idea of a plate, that first emptiness.
She sinks her teeth into the space
between dream and nothing left.
And me, dare I go down on my knees,
tongue straggling, licking the pain away
one slobber at a time? Of course not,
I'm doing my best to hoard my feelings,
the taste of loss pushed into a
corner of my cheek.

How to Hide a Broken Heart

At first it's post-traumatic stress,
memories of the drill smoking,
ivory fragments flying,
latex thumbs pinching back your lips.
Then the ache rises to a throb
like a half-launched rocket.

Of course you don't mention
to your dentist that your heart is
down and wrecked as well, that
love twisted in with its gypsy
fingers, snapping carelessness into
stunned corners, leaving you
susceptible to fevers and feints,
all those naïvetés that make
you squirm like a victim.

Your gums begin to quiet down,
the gleam back in your smile.
Now there's no excuse for the wince,
your heart can no longer pretend
to be a tooth in crisis. You'd better
fetch a hammer, arrange an accident.
Be a broken finger, a blister, a black eye,
something admissible. Shove a sock
where your heart cries and scramble
your face into the beginnings of a twinkle.

One day you'll run out of symptoms
and be nothing less than sick at heart.
I'm broken, the skipped beats will say,
no more need for bacteria, or cankers,

or cancer cells. You'll finally stand there,
chest thrust out, ribs spread, a fractured
sacred space shining with simple misery.
This is who you really are, splinter
among splinters, shard of a shard.

Lucinda Williams Is in Pain

Larynx tearing like a dotted line, half of her
falling to the floor, swept under the saggy couch,
just a crease of her crying shoulder sticking out.
This is cottage country, hearts barbecued here, not broken.
           There must be some mistake.
Beavers swim past the dock with their teeth grinning,
dragonflies imitating turquoise brooches.
Simply not the place for howling, then passing out.
Perhaps a sugared lemonade instead,
a baggy bathing suit, a Colville canoe
sitting on a bestselling copy of itself.
At your most daring, a dusk walk amongst the grasses
that seem to leap like sword-fight ballets in Chinese action films.
No one really hurt, nothing but milkweed and
chicory, and that sweet mix of suntan lotion and
sweat on the skin of someone you'd like to fuck.
Lucinda groans, she's heard that word before, burrs held
to her breasts, deer flies eating soft pieces of her neck.
A synonym for love, a sticky pink case
of poison ivy, an inadvertent scratch.
Should have left lust at home with the bills and the hemorrhoids.
What's it doing here, swimming in the shallows
with those egg-yolk sunfish, darting in slippery
beams of 2:00 p.m., soaking slutty in a hammock?
Someone, drag Lucinda out of here,
her body bruised with tattoos.
Roll her in the trunk, leave her lying drunk on
Highway 7, one thumb cocked in an SOS.
She'll survive: asphalt weed, skank-voiced loon
kicked out of the choir, wound without rhyme or end.
Let's return to dappled, to placid, to sheer.
All you want to hear are the bubbly gurgles of
motorboats, the light-fingered flips of waves, the hushes
of your heart as it tiptoes whole from your chest.

Nice, Nicely

It's all surface structure: nice, nicely,
niceness, everything but a verb.
Shocked to see the wedding photos,
my whole head smiling, even crow's feet
doing their best to look like tickles.
I nice you. Is that really what love's
all about, the golden rule acted out?
Make no mistake, this is so much more
than sweet swipes or a penny's worth
of pleasure. This is sweat provoking,
jaw pounding, the kind of muscle that can
break forks or bend knives into sneers.

One day I will die of too much niceness,
moon-blanched cheeks and lots
of set design. An agreeable corpse,
nerves wired to pat mourners' hands:
Nice of you to come. Instead,
I should be making fists, gripping
the pretty bone of your wrist
and snapping it like the promise
you never meant to keep.
That's what you deserve for loving
the way I loved you
instead of loving me.

None of this is rocketry, I know,
the heart tied down like a hot air
balloon, cumbersome, unsteady.
So where did I pick up the swindle
that nice equals ever after? Suck-up
seems to segue into love.
Novocaine shot directly to the brain –

how painless to lose complete
layers of myself. Next life, we're
switching roles: I'll do the receiving,
you be the smile that slices its way
through all that cutlery and gleam.

The Third Presence

You with your face stuck inside a mirror,
an open window looking out on a world
where you were everything. And me,
staring in at you, a moon nestled
on the windowsill, the big light of admiration.
A perfect twosome, eh? Loved and loving.
Now that it's over, it's not you I worry about,
or even me with my misplaced shine.
But what happened to the blending
of us both, the third presence, that energy
resonating between need and inspire. I picture
a smudge of white against the blueblood sky,
something that can almost be wiped away.
I've lost a sense of myself, my shadow unstitched
and slipping into every crack. There's a loneliness
out there that doesn't know its own worth,
a darkness wild for any kind of bright.

I take walks every afternoon, hoping to find
something I recognize in the certain pink
of a stranger's face or a groan in the space
between my own familiar breaths. But every
happenstance pulses with an odd newness,
one experimental poem after another – a tree
in the shape of a startled crow, a license plate
making gibberish of the alphabet,
a handmade sign on a hydro pole
proclaiming a lostness named Lucy.
No evidence of anything that looks like me.
In fact, the only constant is the weaving line
of footprints in the snow behind me, evidence
of intention, a dogged state of desire.
Could it be that loneliness is stalking me,
or am I continuing to shed bits of it
all over the place? Am I mistaking myself
for someone who deserves a following?

Rilke asks if the earth knows me,
and I have to shake my head. It appears
that I'm the man in the moon and will shine
on absolutely anything. I'm the one who
paints windowsills white, who slips midnight
mirrors their ghosting. And I'm the one
who loved you knowing full well
you'd never love me back. A martyr,
a fool – how easy it is to name
a sunspot *blindness*. That loneliness
is right here on the page, in the way
the words relate to one another, a wariness
that makes a feeble kind of music,
afraid to come right out and cry.
The third presence is who I am now,
the old me so bruised and tattered
that it simply fades away. In the daylight,
it's hard to tell the difference, but look
closely, the scars where you used to begin
or end – I forget which – the stitching
where my shadow can be ripped off, there,
see, the new sheen, that slight rippling
where the skin hasn't yet settled over bone.

Acknowledgements

Much appreciation to the editors of the magazines where many of these poems first saw light: *Border Crossings, Canadian Literature, The Comstock Review, CV2, The Dalhousie Review, Eleven Eleven Event, The Fiddlehead, FreeFall, Grain, How the Light Gets In: An Authology of Contemporary Poetry from Canada, The Literary Review, Misunderstandings Magazine, The Nashwaak Review, paperplates, PRECEIPICe PRISM international, Saranac Review.*

My gratitude to all those whose unconditional love makes such a difference. First and foremost, Karen Dempster, whose generosity and understanding keep my heart spinning. Huge thanks to Don McKay, whose faith and encouragement continue to be a great gift in my life. And Alayna Munce, whose copy-editing is a wonder to behold. Hugs to both my writing groups: the irreplaceable Carol Gall, Hyacinthe Miller, and Sharon Wilston; and the Thursday night angels, Maureen Harris, Maureen Hynes, Jim Nason, and Liz Ukrainetz. And to Phil Hall, Jeanette Lynes, and Naomi Shihab Nye for words beyond the call of duty. I also owe so much to the courage and caring of the Aceti family, Roo Borson, Allan Briesmaster, Sheila Dalton, Don Domanski, Lorri Neilsen Glenn, the Hayes family, Bruce Hunter, Julia McCarthy, Karen McElrea, John Reibetanz, the Rodaro family, Isabelle Saunders, Russell Thornton, the Vanderlip family, and Jan Zwicky – thank you for listening and lasting.

Three cheers for the pleasure of the Brick Books experience. Don, Stan, Kitty, Maureen, Alayna – extraordinary friends and supporters. Bravo to Alan Siu at Sunville for the gorgeous design job. Finally, thank you to the amazing artist Tony Scherman for his brazen "Jocasta."

Barry Dempster is the author of nine previous collections of poetry, the most recent of which, *The Burning Alphabet* (Brick Books), was nominated for the Governor General's Award and won the Canadian Authors' Association Jack Chalmers Award. He is also the author of a children's book, two volumes of short stories and a novel, *The Ascension of Jesse Rapture* (Quarry Press). Born and raised in Toronto, he now lives in Holland Landing, Ontario, where he runs a film series, two book clubs and a writing group.